MW01600997

# Notes From My Father:

## FOUNDATIONS FOR SUCCESSFUL LIVING

**WORKBOOK AND STUDY GUIDE**

# NOTES FROM MY FATHER:

Foundations for Successful Living

Study Guide and Work Book

## DR. STEVE E. WHEELER

Copyright 2025

Scripture marked AMP are from the Amplified Bible Copyright © 2015 by The Lockman Foundation, La Habra, CA 90631. All rights reserved.

Scripture marked AMPC are from the Amplified Bible, Classic Edition Copyright © 1954, 1958, 1962, 1964, 1965, 1987 by The Lockman Foundation.

Scripture marked CEV are from the Contemporary English Version Copyright © 1995 by American Bible Society For more information about CEV, visit www.bibles.com and www.cev.bible.

Scripture marked EASY are from the Easy English Bible Copyright © MissionAssist 2019 - Charitable Incorporated Organisation 1162807. Used by permission. All rights reserved.

Scripture marked ERV are from the Easy-to-Read Version Copyright © 2006 by Bible League International.

Scripture marked ESV are from The Holy Bible, English Standard Version. ESV® Text Edition: 2016. Copyright © 2001 by Crossway Bibles, a publishing ministry of Good News Publishers.

Scripture marked GNT are from the Good News Translation (Today's English Version, Second Edition) Copyright © 1992 American Bible Society. All rights reserved.

Scripture marked GW are from God's Word Translation Copyright © 1995, 2003, 2013, 2014, 2019, 2020 by God's Word to the Nations Mission Society. All rights reserved.

Scripture quotations marked MSG are taken from *THE MESSAGE*, copyright © 1993, 2002, 2018 by Eugene H. Peterson. Used by permission of NavPress. All rights reserved. Represented by Tyndale House Publishers, Inc.

Scripture marked NCV are taken from the New Century Version®. Copyright © 2005 by Thomas Nelson. Used by permission. All rights reserved.

Scripture marked NIV are from THE HOLY BIBLE, NEW INTERNATIONAL VERSION®, NIV® Copyright © 1973, 1978, 1984, 2011 by Biblica, Inc.® Used by permission. All rights reserved worldwide.

Scripture marked NKJV are from the New King James Version®. Copyright © 1982 by Thomas Nelson. Used by permission. All rights reserved.

Scripture quotations marked NLT are taken from the *Holy Bible*, New Living Translation, copyright © 1996, 2004, 2015 by Tyndale House Foundation. Used by permission of Tyndale House Publishers, Inc., Carol Stream, Illinois 60188. All rights reserved.

Scripture quotations marked NLV are taken from the *New Life Version*, copyright © 1969 and 2003. Used by permission of Barbour Publishing, Inc., Uhrichsville, Ohio 44683. All rights reserved.

Scripture marked NOG is from the Names of God version GOD'S WORD®, © 1995 God's Word to the Nations. Used by permission of Baker Publishing Group.

Scripture marked PHILLIPS are from The New Testament in Modern English by J.B Phillips copyright © 1960, 1972 J. B. Phillips. Administered by The Archbishops' Council of the Church of England. Used by Permission.

Scripture marked TLB are from The Living Bible copyright © 1971 by Tyndale House Foundation. Used by permission of Tyndale House Publishers Inc., Carol Stream, Illinois 60188. All rights reserved.

Scripture quotations marked TPT are from The Passion Translation®. Copyright © 2017, 2018, 2020 by Passion & Fire Ministries, Inc. Used by permission. All rights reserved. ThePassionTranslation.com.

Scripture marked VOICE are taken from The Voice™. Copyright © 2008 by Ecclesia Bible Society. Used by permission. All rights reserved.

ISBN: 979-8-9992141-3-3

Library of Congress: 2025912310

Printed in the United States of America

Cover Design:

Nathan Atwood

Published by WheelerMediaGroup

405 Indigo Springs St.

Henderson, NV 89014

# Also by Dr. Steve E. Wheeler

*Adventures of Faith:*

Available on Amazon

*Through the Shadows: Overcoming Fear in the Midst of a Pandemic*:

Available on Amazon

*To Grace and Sarah, our beloved children. This book is written specifically for you and those who will come after you. Each sentence is carefully chosen. Each subject is written about thoughtfully and prayerfully, prompted, we believe, by the Holy Spirit. Our goal is to empower you to live the best life God has planned for you. Your mom and I are so very proud of you, and we are blessed that God has chosen us to be your parents and to prepare you for a life of success.*

*To our descendants—our grandchildren, great-grandchildren, and great-great-grandchildren. Even though we may not have met some of you in person, we have held you close to our hearts. We have prayed for you, declaring that you become righteous and godly individuals, fulfilling God's unique purpose for each of you. May the stories of our successes and challenges inspire and embolden you to wholeheartedly commit your lives to God.*

*In these pages, you will find the principles your mom and I lived by. Some of these principles we were very good at living out in our daily lives. Others were principles we were striving to improve upon. Looking back over our lives, we feel the foundations and principles found in this book are the ones you can build successful lives upon.*

*This is also dedicated to you, the reader. My prayer is that you will find this book helpful as you seek to guide your children and raise them in the way they should go. My prayer is this book will be a guide for you as you seek your family tree for generations to come.*

# Acknowledgments

First and foremost, I want to thank Jesus, my personal Lord and Savior. Thank You, Holy Spirit, for the inspiration to write this book and for the wisdom and insight You have given me. The final product of this book is a little different from what it started out to be, and I am thankful.

I want to thank my precious wife, Veronica. You played an important role in the completion of this book. Thank you for your wisdom and insight as you read and reread this manuscript. I love you more than words can express. Jesus has given us a wonderful and exciting life, and I'm thrilled we get to spend the rest of our lives together serving the Lord together.

Thank you to my girls, Grace and Sarah. This book is yours, written specifically for you and the generations that will follow after you. It is such a joy and honor to be your dad, and I love you both so very much.

To Janet Meyers, who, as always, gave me encouragement while writing this book. She also did some editing for this book as well. Our family is thankful God put such a mighty woman of God in our family.

# Contents

# A Note From The Author

This study guide is great for personal use or for a small group setting. It is also a great tool for your family, which you can use to begin to teach your children the foundations for a successful life. Inside these pages, you will find discussion questions, reflection questions, Scripture passages, and prayers.

# Part I:

## STEWARDSHIP

ONE

# Stewardship

The author introduces this book by addressing stewardship. He states everything will rise and fall based upon how we view stewardship and managing what God has placed in our hands. As you read and reflect, ask the Holy Spirit to speak to you in this area. Allow Him to search your heart and bring to light anything that may be hindering you from stepping into your role as a steward.

**Discussion Questions:**

1. How do you view the principle of stewardship?

_____

_____

_____

_____

2. Do you view yourself as an owner or a manager of the things God has placed in your hands? Why?

_____

_____

_____

_____

3. In what ways have you personally struggled with stewardship in your life?

_____

_____

_____

_____

## **Scripture:**

### Matthew 25:14–30 NLT:

*"Again, the Kingdom of Heaven can be illustrated by the story of a man going on a long trip. He called together his servants and entrusted his money to them while he was gone. He gave five bags of silver to one, two bags of silver to another, and one bag of silver to the last—dividing it in proportion to their abilities. He then left on his trip.*

*The servant who received the five bags of silver began to invest the money and earned five more. The servant with two bags of silver also went to work and earned two more. But the servant who received the one bag of silver dug a hole in the ground and hid the master's money.*

*After a long time their master returned from his trip and called them to give an account of how they had used his money. The servant to whom he had entrusted the five bags of silver came forward with five more and said, 'Master, you gave me five bags of silver to invest, and I have earned five more.*

*The master was full of praise. 'Well done, my good and faithful servant. You have been faithful in handling this small amount, so now I will give you many more responsibilities. Let's celebrate together!*

*The servant who had received the two bags of silver came forward and said, 'Master, you gave me two bags of silver to invest, and I have earned two more.'*

*The master said, 'Well done, my good and faithful servant. You have been faithful in handling this small amount, so now I will give you many more responsibilities. Let's celebrate together!*

*Then the servant with the one bag of silver came and said, 'Master, I knew you were a harsh man, harvesting crops you didn't plant and gathering crops you didn't cultivate. I was afraid I would lose your money, so I hid it in the earth. Look, here is your money back.'*

*But the master replied, 'You wicked and lazy servant! If you knew I harvested crops I didn't plant and gathered crops I didn't cultivate, why didn't you deposit my money in the bank? At least I could have gotten some interest on it.'*

*Then he ordered, 'Take the money from this servant, and give it to the one with the ten bags of silver. To those who use well what they are given, even more will be given, and they will have an abundance. But from those who do nothing, even what little they have will be taken away. Now throw this useless servant into outer darkness, where there will be weeping and gnashing of teeth.'"*

Genesis 1:26−28 Voice:

*"Now let Us conceive a new creation—humanity--made in Our image, fashioned according to Our likeness. And let Us grant them authority over all the earth—the fish in the sea and the birds in the sky, the domesticated animals and the small creeping creatures on the earth. So God did just that. He created humanity in His image, created them male and female. Then God blessed them and gave them this directive: 'Be fruitful and multiply. Populate the earth. I make you trustees of My estate, so care for My creation and rule over the fish of the sea, the birds of the sky, and every creature that roams across the earth.'"*

## Reflection Questions:

1. As you read this Scripture about the parable of the talents, look at the three levels of stewardship mentioned. As you reflect on your life, where do you see yourself as a steward? Do you see yourself as the person with five talents who traded and made another five? Or the two who also gained two more? Or do you see yourself as the steward who, because he was afraid, kept what he had been given?

_____

_____

_____

_____

2. Do you see yourself as a steward over God's estate? Why or why not?

_____

_____

_____

_____

## **Action Step:**

1. What practical steps can you take today to help you become a better steward of the resources God has given you?

_____

_____

_____

_____

_____

*Prayer:*

*Jesus, I come and humble myself before You. I confess I have not been a good steward of the things You have placed in my life. I have not had the proper understanding of stewardship and the role I play in managing the assets You have given me. I repent and ask You to forgive me. Open my heart and eyes to see Your truth and help me be a doer of the Word.*

*In Your name, I pray. Amen.*

# TWO

# Tithing
_____

Proverbs 3:9−10 TLB:
*"Honor the Lord by giving him the first part of all your income, and he will fill your barns with wheat and barley and overflow your wine vats with the finest wines."*

D r. Steve writes in the book that one of the most important foundations of stewardship is the tithe. Everything else that touches our lives will rest on our ability to trust God with our money. In reality, *we do not truly own our wealth.* We are stewards entrusted with money and riches by God. As stewards, God trusts us to use our money for His glory.

## Discussion Questions:

1. Do you believe tithing is relevant as a New Testament believer? Why or why not?

_____
_____
_____
_____

2. Why do you think tithing is so powerful?

_____

_____

_____

_____

## Scripture:

Malachi 3:8-12 GNT:

*"I ask you, is it right for a person to cheat God? Of course not, yet you are cheating me. 'How?' you ask. In the matter of tithes and offerings. A curse is on all of you because the whole nation is cheating me. Bring the full amount of your tithes to the Temple, so that there will be plenty of food there. Put me to the test and you will see that I will open the windows of heaven and pour out on you in abundance all kinds of good things. I will not let insects destroy your crops, and your grapevines will be loaded with grapes. Then the people of all nations will call you happy, because your land will be a good place to live."*

## Reflection Questions:

1. When have you ever struggled with giving your tithe?

_____

_____

_____

_____

2. If you have struggled with giving your tithe, what was the motivation of your heart? Greed? Insecurity? Fear?

_____

_____

_____

_____

3. Do you find it difficult to trust God with your finances? Why do you think the reason is?

_____

_____

_____

_____

## **Action Steps:**

1. What steps can you take this week to deal with the underlying heart issues you may face about trusting God with your finances?

_____

_____

_____

_____

2. In what practical ways can you become a better steward of your finances?

_____

_____

_____

_____

---

*Prayer:*

*Lord, I come to You, and I ask You to change my heart. Help me let go of the fear and insecurity that keeps me from fully trusting You with my life and finances. Give me revelation and insight into Your Word, and let Your Word change my life.*

*In Jesus Name, I pray,*

*Amen*

# THREE

## Open Hands / Open Heart

Deuteronomy 15:11 NIV:
*"There will always be poor in the land. Therefore I command you to be openhanded towards your brothers and toward the poor and needy in your land."*

It's important to live our lives holding things loosely, with an open hand. An open hand lets go of things rather than holding on for dear life. Do your hands reflect an open heart by generously giving to those in need? Having an open heart will lead to having an open hand. When we live with an open hand, God can bless us, and He can use us to bless others.

### Discussion Questions:

1. How have you recently been stretched in your faith and obedience in your generosity?

_____

_____

_____

_____

2. Describe a time when your hands and heart were closed in the area of giving.

_____

_____

_____

_____

## Scripture:

### Psalm 104:28 TLB:

*"You supply it, and they gather it. You open wide your hand to feed them, and they are satisfied with all your bountiful provision."*

## Reflection Questions:

1. Imagine what your life would look like if you lived with open hands.

_____

_____

_____

_____

2. What would you do if your needs were met, and you had enough to give to those in need?

_____

_____

_____

_____

## Action Step:

1. Ask the Lord if there is something in your hand that He would want you to give away.

_____

_____

_____

_____

Notes From My Father:

*Prayer:*
*Lord, I haven't always lived life with an open hand. There have been times when my heart was closed, and I was disobedient to Your leading. I repent and ask You to change my heart. Amen.*

# FOUR

# Generosity

Proverbs 11:24–29 TPT:
*"Generosity brings prosperity, but withholding from charity brings poverty. Those who live to bless others will have blessings heaped upon them, and the one who pours out his life to pour out blessings will be saturated with favor."*

Generosity is being open and willing to share with others without the expectation of receiving something back in return. Sharing what we have is the simplest expression of generosity, whether it is money from our pocket or food for a homeless person.

## Discussion Questions:

1. In what ways do you find it difficult to be generous with your finances?

_____

_____

_____

_____

2. How have you seen God provide for you as a result of your generosity?

_____

_____

_____

_____

## Scripture:

1 Timothy 6:17–19 MSG:
*"Tell those rich in this world's wealth to quit being so full of themselves and so obsessed with money, which is here today and gone tomorrow. Tell them to go after God, who piles on all the riches we could ever manage-to do good, to be rich in helping others, to be extravagantly generous."*

## Reflection Questions:

1. As you read this Scripture, imagine what it would be like to be extravagantly generous with your finances. How would your life be different?

_____

_____

_____

_____

2. What would it take for you to step out in faith and begin to be extravagantly generous?

_____

_____

_____

_____

## Action Steps:

1. Pray and ask the Holy Spirit to speak to you in the area of generosity. Ask Him what He would like you to do, and then be obedient to what He speaks.

_____

_____

_____

2. Keep a journal of how the Lord uses you to be a blessing to others and how the Lord provides for you.

_____

_____

_____

_____

———————

*Prayer:*

*Lord, I want to live a life that is pleasing to You. Help me live a life of generosity. Show me ways I can be generous to others. Thank You for putting resources into my hands that I can share with others. Amen.*

# FIVE

# Greed

_____

Proverbs 28:25 Voice:
*"When the greedy want more, they stir up trouble; but when a person trusts in the Eternal, he's sure to prosper."*

When someone is greedy, they have an unquenchable thirst for money that leads them to sacrifice their morals for it. Greed may seem promising, but it can never provide true satisfaction, and the effects of greed can lead us into poverty.

## Discussion Questions:

1. The author mentions some factors that lead to greed, such as envy or insecurity, trauma, or unfulfilled needs. In what ways have you struggled with greed, and what do you think were the underlying causes?

_____

_____

_____

_____

2. How do you overcome greed?

_____

_____

_____

_____

Ecclesiastes 5:10 NLT:
*"Those who love money will never have enough. How meaningless to think that wealth brings true happiness!"*

## Reflection Question:

1. The author shares how greed revealed the condition of his heart. When you think about your life, what does the Holy Spirit reveal to you about the condition of your heart?

_____

_____

_____

_____

## Action Step:

2. Pray and ask God to show you what you may need to do to break the power of greed in your life.

_____

_____

_____

_____

*Prayer:*
*Lord, I have been fearful and insecure about my finances. I confess I haven't trusted You with my life. I repent and ask for forgiveness. Help me, Lord, to overcome greed and its effects in my life. Thank You for hearing and answering my prayer. Amen.*

SIX

# Debt

Romans 13:8 AMPC:
*"...Keep out of debt and owe no man anything."*

D r. Steve writes that 61 percent of Americans (three out of five people) are in debt, owing an average of $5,875. He writes that 48 percent of Americans depend on their credit card to cover essential living expenses. It is estimated that fifty-nine percent of Millennials use credit cards for living expenses.

## Discussion Questions:

1. Why is debt a form of slavery?

_____

_____

_____

_____

2. Do you currently have debt? If so, do you have a plan to eliminate it? If not, what are you doing to stay out of debt?

_____

_____

_____

_____


1 Timothy 5:8 Voice:
*"And listen, if someone is not providing for his own relatives and especially his own household, then he is denying the faith and is worse off than an unbeliever."*

## Reflection Question:

1. Think of where you are financially. Has debt hindered your ability to be generous and provide for your family?

_____

_____

_____

_____


## Action Steps:

1. List all your debts, from smallest to largest, and ask God to show you how to pay those debts off.

_____

_____

_____

_____


2. Write down the plan the Lord gave you and begin the journey to financial freedom.

_____

_____

_____

_____

3. If you are married, do this together as a couple and come into agreement that you will be debt-free.

_____

_____

_____

_____

4. Create a budget and begin to live by it.

_____

_____

_____

_____

*Prayer:*

*Jesus, debt is a curse, and I know You do not want me to live under a curse. Give me a plan to tackle my debt. Give me creative ideas to earn extra income to pay off our debt. I want to experience the life You died to give me. Thank You, Jesus, for hearing and answering my prayer. Amen.*

# SEVEN

## Stewarding Our Gifts and Talents

1 Peter 4:10 TPT:
*"Every believer has received grace gifts, so use them to serve one another as faithful stewards of the many-colored tapestry of God's grace."*

The book talks about stewarding our lives and the gifts and talents God has placed inside each of us. The Bible says that before we were even born, He knew us and formed us in our mother's womb. He placed gifts and talents within us when He created us.

### Discussion Questions:

1. What natural talents and abilities has God given you?

_____

_____

_____

_____

2. What spiritual gifts has He given you?

_____

_____

_____

_____

1 Corinthians 4:2 NKJV:
*"Moreover it is required in stewards that one be found faithful."*

## Reflection Questions:

1. Do you think you are being a good steward of the gifts, talents, and abilities God has given you? Why or why not?

_____

_____

_____

_____

2. How are you cultivating and growing in your giftings?

_____

_____

_____

_____

## Action Steps:

1. Ask God to reveal your hidden gifts, anointings, and talents you may not be aware of.

_____

_____

_____

_____

2. Seek the Lord and ask Him how you can grow and mature in those gifts.

_____

_____

_____

_____

*Prayer:*
*Lord, reveal to me what gifts You have placed inside me. Show me how to cultivate those gifts and use them for Your glory. Amen.*

# Part II:

INHERITANCE

EIGHT

# Financial Inheritance

Proverbs 13:22 NKJV:
*"A good man leaves an inheritance to his children's children."*

The book talks about generational wealth, and the author writes that generational wealth was a new concept for him. He writes that God is a generational God, and He desires for families and their values to continue for generations.

**Discussion Questions:**

1. Is the idea of building generational wealth a new concept for you? Why or why not?

_____

_____

_____

_____

2. What family values are you passing down to your children?

_____
_____
_____
_____

Deuteronomy 6:5−9 Voice:

*"You should love Him, your True God, with all your heart and soul, with every ounce of your strength. Make the things I'm commanding you today part of who you are. Repeat them to your children. Talk about them when you're sitting together in your home and when you're walking together down the road. Make them the last thing you talk about before you go to bed and the first thing you talk about the next morning."*

## Reflection Questions:

1. Imagine the generations that will follow after you. What values, ethics, and standards of what it means to be a part of your family do you want to see them live?

_____
_____
_____
_____

2. If you haven't done so, think about what is important to you and write down your family values.

_____
_____
_____
_____

## Action Steps:

1. Develop a strategy to impart your family values into the lives of your children.

_____
_____
_____

2. Begin to teach and train your children to live by those values. Demonstrate them by the way you live and teach them to your children.

_____

_____

_____

_____

———————————

*Prayer:*

*Jesus, we ask for Your wisdom as we develop our family values. Give us a strategy on how we are to train our children in these values. Thank You, Jesus. Amen.*

# NINE

# Generational Wealth

Proverbs 13:22 Voice:
*"A good person leaves an inheritance for his grandchildren, but the wealth of the sinner is eventually passed on to the right-living."*

The Bible says we are called to manage wealth for God's glory, and it is a good thing to pass that wealth to the next generation. Our vision is to leave a legacy of purpose and generational wealth. We want to make sure the generations that follow us will manage wealth God's way.

Building generational wealth is all about having God's perspective on your life. God cares about generations. God designed us to live a purposeful life and leave a legacy, so we must move from having a *lifetime perspective* into a *generational perspective*.

## Discussion Questions:

1. What do you need to do differently to plan how you will pass your wealth down to your children and your future generations?

_____

_____

_____

_____

2. What's the difference between having a *lifetime* perspective and a *generational* perspective?

_____

_____

_____

_____

Proverb 22:6 NCV:
*"Train children to live the right way, and when they are old, they will not stray from it."*

## Reflection Questions:

1. Think about your children and your children's children. How would you want them to live their lives?

_____

_____

_____

_____

2. How will you teach your children and their children to manage the wealth you pass on?

_____

_____

_____

_____

## Action Step:

1. Create a plan to instill financial responsibility into your children and strive to teach them the importance of money and how to manage it.

_____

_____

_____

_____

Notes From My Father:

*Prayer:*

*Lord, help us teach our children to be responsible with money and how to manage the wealth we will pass down to them. Give us Your insight and wisdom and help us develop a plan to create and pass our wealth down to our children. Amen.*

## TEN

# Family Values

Deuteronomy 6:6 Voice:
*"Make the things I'm commanding you today part of who you are."*

The author writes he had a hard time with the concept of family values. No written values were passed down to him that he was expected to live by. Before he and his wife married, they talked about their family histories and how they wanted to change their family tree, beginning with them and then flowing down to future generations.

### Discussion Questions:

1. What comes to mind with the idea of family values?

_____

_____

_____

_____

2. What are some things that make up your family values?

_____

_____

_____

_____

3. In what ways do you want your children's lives to be better than yours?

_____

_____

_____

_____

Genesis 18:19 ERV:

*"I have made a special agreement with him. I did this so that he would command his children and his descendants to live the way the LORD wants them to. I did this so that they would live right and be fair. Then I, the LORD, can give him what I promised."*

**Reflection Questions:**

1. What values were passed down to you from your parents?

_____

_____

_____

_____

2. What values do you desire to pass on to your children?

_____

_____

_____

_____

**Action Step:**

1. Write down what things you can do together as a family that will reinforce your family identity and what you desire your family to be.

_____

_____

_____

_____

Notes From My Father:

*Prayer:*

*Teach us, Lord, the importance of having a vision for our family. Help us recognize what we desire to be as a family that will impact future generations. We want to leave a lasting legacy for our children's children to live by. Thank You, Jesus, for giving us Your wisdom in the area. Amen.*

ELEVEN

# Building a Spiritual Legacy

Psalm 145:4 NLV:
*"Families of this time will praise Your works to the families-to-come. They will tell about Your powerful acts."*

The Bible places great value on knowing our family history, especially our roots of faith. The stories of those who have come before us can strengthen and encourage our faith today. The most valuable heirloom we can pass down to our children and future generations is a legacy of faith. We want to build a family heritage, a spiritual legacy that will last for generations.

**Discussion Questions:**

1. The author talks about "spiritual markers." What is your understanding of this concept?

_____

_____

_____

_____

2. What are some spiritual markers in your lives? What things do they remind you of?

_____

_____

_____

_____

2 Timothy 1:5 Voice:
*"What strikes me most is how natural and sincere your faith is. I am convinced that the same faith that dwelt in your grandmother, Lois, and your mother, Eunice, abides in you as well."*

**Reflection Questions:**

1. In what ways can you start building a spiritual legacy?

_____

_____

_____

_____

2. Are you modeling a life of faith to your children? What do you need to change?

_____

_____

_____

_____

**Action Step:**

1. Begin a journey of writing down the spiritual markers you want the future generations of your family to remember.

_____

_____

_____

_____

Notes From My Father:

*Prayer:*
*Thank You for the things You have done in our lives. Thank You that we have spiritual markers we can pass down to future generations of our family. Jesus, we want to build a lasting spiritual legacy that will impact future generations! Amen.*

# Part III:

INTEGRITY

TWELVE

# Integrity Is Inconvenient

Proverbs 20:7 AMP:
*"The righteous man who walks in integrity and lives life in accord with his [godly] beliefs
—How blessed [happy and spiritually secure] are his children after him [who have his
example to follow]."*

Integrity is inconvenient. It always costs you something to be a man or woman of integrity. Being a person of integrity is something you will have to work on daily. Integrity will always kill the flesh!

**Discussion Questions:**

1. How has it cost you to be a man or woman of integrity?

_____

_____

_____

_____

2. Share a time when you had to make a sacrifice to uphold your integrity.

_____

_____

_____

_____

Proverbs 20:7 NLT:
*"The godly walk with integrity; blessed are their children who follow them."*

### Reflection Questions:

1. Pause for a moment and reflect on your life right now. Are you walking with integrity? Why or why not?

_____

_____

_____

_____

2. Is there an aspect of your life where you need to improve your integrity?

_____

_____

_____

_____

### Action Step:

1. Integrity starts with the small things in life. Write down one or two areas where you will walk with integrity.

_____

_____

_____

_____

*Prayer:*
*Lord, I desire to be a person of integrity. Holy Spirit, shine Your light in my heart and reveal to me where I start walking with integrity. Help me to live my life as You want me to. Amen.*

THIRTEEN

# Keeping Your Word

Psalm 15:1−2, 5 MSG:
*"God, who gets invited to your dinner place? How do we get on your guest list? Walk straight, act right, tell the truth... Keep your word even when it costs you..."*

The author shares his testimony of when he was a young man, saying that keeping his word was not important to him. His reputation among friends and family was, "You can't believe anything Steve says. You can't trust a word he speaks." He pretended he didn't care, but deep down inside, it bothered him greatly.

## Discussion Questions:

1. How well do you do with keeping your word?

_____

_____

_____

_____

2. Is there an area where you have not kept your word that you need to change?

_____

_____

_____

_____

Matthew 5:37 TLB:
"Say just a simple 'Yes, I will' or 'No, I won't.' Your word is enough. To strengthen your promise with a vow shows that something is wrong."

## Reflection Question:

1. Think about your life and relationships. Honestly, ask yourself if those in your circle of influence trust you. Do they trust your word?

_____

_____

_____

_____

## Action Step:

1. Ask the Holy Spirit to reveal areas in your life where you have not consistently kept your word. Write them down and ask Him to help you change.

_____

_____

_____

_____

*Prayer:*
*Jesus, I desire to be a person of my word. I want people to trust me when I say I will do something. I know keeping my word can sometimes be painful, so help me have the strength to say what I mean and mean what I say. I pray in Jesus' name. Amen.*

# FOURTEEN

# Dependability

Hebrews 13:8 VOICE:
*"Jesus the Anointed One is always the same: yesterday, today, and forever."*

Dependability is one attribute of integrity. It is the quality of being trustworthy and reliable—the quality of being able to be relied upon. Being a dependable person means we do what we say we will do, and we are worthy of trust.

## Discussion Questions:

1. What do others say about you? Do they say you are dependable?

_____

_____

_____

_____

2. Dependability involves consistency. As you examine your life, do you find you are consistent?

_____

_____

_____

_____

Hebrews 13:8 EASY:
*"Jesus Christ is always the same, yesterday, today and for ever."*

## Reflection Question:

1. Looking over your life and relationships, would you say you consistently follow through on the commitments you make?

_____

_____

_____

_____

## Action Step:

1. If you find that you fall short in this area, repent and ask God to help you become dependable.

_____

_____

_____

_____

Prayer:
*I humble myself before You, Lord, and I ask that You help me in this area of being dependable. I want people to be able to put their trust in me and believe my words. Thank You for changing my character. Amen.*

# FIFTEEN

# Honesty

2 Corinthians 8:21 NLV:
*"We want to do the right thing. We want God and men to know that we are honest."*

Honesty is described in the dictionary as always telling the truth and never stealing or cheating. Honesty is also marked by being free from deceit or untruthfulness and being sincere. Honesty is not just about truth-telling; it is about truth-living. We live our lives honestly before the Lord and before people.

## Discussion Questions:

1. Can you share a time when being truthful and honest caused you pain?

_____

_____

_____

_____

2. What fruit was produced in you as you walked through that experience?

_____

_____

_____

_____

Proverbs 12:17 ERV:
*"Good people speak the truth and can be trusted in court, but liars make bad witnesses."*

## Reflection Question:

1. Would you say you live life honestly before the Lord and before people? If not, how can you make a change in this area?

_____

_____

_____

_____

## Action Step:

1. Pray and ask the Holy Spirit to put His finger on something in your life that He wants to become more like Him.

_____

_____

_____

_____

*Prayer:*
*Lord, my desire is to walk humbly before You with an open heart. I desire to be known as a person who is honest and truthful. Help me always to live a life that is pleasing before You.*
*Amen.*

# SIXTEEN

# Loyalty

2 Chronicles 16:9 GNT:

*"The LORD keeps close watch over the whole world, to give strength to those whose hearts are loyal to him..."*

Loyalty is a greatly needed quality in the world today. It's important to not only teach, but also to demonstrate loyalty to our children. Having a loyal heart is one that is faithful to God. Being loyal exhibits our commitment to Christ by our commitment to people.

## Discussion Questions:

1. Do you agree with the author that loyalty is in short supply these days? Why or why not?

_____

_____

_____

_____

2. Share some examples of people who have been loyal to you and how that made you feel.

_____

_____

_____

_____

Proverbs 20:6 TLB:
*"Most people will tell you what loyal friends they are, but are they telling the truth?"*

## Reflection Question:

1. How can you develop the attribute of loyalty?

_____

_____

_____

_____

## Action Step:

1. Ask the Lord to show you how to show loyalty to those He has placed in your life.

_____

_____

_____

_____

*Prayer:*
*Heavenly Father, my life is an open book before You. You know my coming and going and my innermost thoughts. Give me wisdom and revelation in this area of loyalty. Help me make the adjustments necessary to enable me to become loyal not only to You but also to those who are in my life. In Jesus' name, I pray. Amen.*

# Part IV:

CHARACTER

# SEVENTEEN

# Character

1 Timothy 4:12 NLV:

*"Let no one show you little respect because you are young. Show other Christians how to live by your life. They should be able to follow you in the way you talk and in what you do. Show them how to live in faith and in love and in holy living."*

Character matters. How you live your life is important. People are watching us, and it is imperative that we set an example by modeling what character is to others. Character can be defined as moral excellence and firmness. Character is what you are when no one is looking.

## Discussion Questions:

1. In what ways have the choices you have made in life developed your character?

_____

_____

_____

_____

2. How have you struggled in the area of character?

_____

_____

_____

_____

### Ruth 3:11 GW:

*"Don't be afraid, my daughter. I will do whatever you say. The whole town knows that you are a woman who has* **strength of character.***"*

## Reflection Question:

1. Developing a godly character always involves choice. What choices can you make today that will affect your character in a positive way?

_____

_____

_____

_____

## Action Step:

1. Ask the Holy Spirit to give you one thing to apply to your life this week that will shape your character.

_____

_____

_____

_____

*Prayer:*
*Father, I want to be a person who exhibits godly character. I want my life to be a reflection of You. Holy Spirit, I ask that You come and sanctify my heart and life, so that I can live a life that is pleasing to You. In Jesus' name, I pray. Amen.*

# EIGHTEEN

# Your Associations

1 Corinthians 15:33 NLV:
*"Do not let anyone fool you. Bad people can make those who want to live good become bad."*

Like it or not, we are known by the company we keep. This means a person will become like the people they choose to spend time with. They will have the same character and moral standards as those they choose to surround themselves with. So, who we have in our lives and who we associate with is extremely important.

## Discussion Questions:

1. Do you have the three types of relationship circles the author writes about?

_____

_____

_____

_____

2. Have you had someone who influenced you negatively? What was the result?

_____

_____

_____

_____

Proverbs 13:20 NLT:

*"Walk with the wise and become wise; associate with fools and get in trouble."*

## Reflection Questions:

1. Do you have someone in your life acting as a mentor to you? If not, who is the Lord directing you to?

_____

_____

_____

_____

2. Do you have someone in your life you are actively mentoring? If not, how can you reach out to someone?

_____

_____

_____

_____

## Action Step:

1. Talk to the Lord about your present circle of relationships. Is there someone you may want to distance yourself from? Is there someone you may want to draw closer to?

_____

_____

_____

_____

Notes From My Father:

*Prayer:*

*Jesus, help me reexamine my relationships. Show me those in my circle of influence who You put into my life to mentor me. Show me who I can mentor and influence for Your glory. Show me who I may want to distance myself from. In Jesus' name, I pray. Amen.*

# NINETEEN

# Your Reputation

Ecclesiastes 7:1 MSG:
*"A good reputation is better than a fat bank account."*

The author writes that your reputation is your most valuable asset. When we hear a name, images of that person and what he or she is immediately spring to mind. Reputation is what people think or believe about you. Their perception may not be accurate, but they believe it is.

## Discussion Questions:

1. Talk about the two ways the author mentions to keep and maintain your good reputation.

_____

_____

_____

_____

2. Are you known as a person who keeps their word? Why or why not?

_____

_____

_____

_____

3. Are you a person who doesn't bend on your convictions? Do you keep the standards you have set for yourself? What do you need to change?

_____

_____

_____

_____

Proverbs 22:1 NLT:

*"Choose a good reputation over great riches; being held in high esteem is better than silver or gold."*

### Reflection Questions:

1. Reflect and take an honest look at your life. What do you think your reputation is with other people?

_____

_____

_____

_____

2. When other people hear your name, what do you imagine they think or believe about you?

_____

_____

_____

_____

### Action Step:

1. Pray and ask the Lord to reveal to you any area in your life He wants to change. If your reputation isn't what it should be, ask the Holy Spirit to show you what you need to do.

_____

_____

_____

_____

Notes From My Father:

*Prayer:*
*Father, thank You for Your love. Thank You for loving me where I am, and thank You for helping me grow into the person You want me to be. I desire to have a good reputation among people. I ask the Holy Spirit to help me become the person You want me to be.*
*Amen.*

TWENTY

# Failure

Psalm 145:14 NCV:
*"The Lord helps those who have been defeated and takes care of those who are in trouble."*

Failure is painful and something everyone experiences in life. Although it is often seen as a negative and discouraging experience, it is an essential part of our personal growth and success. How we respond to failure will determine our course of life.

## Discussion Questions:

1. Think of an instance where you failed. Looking back in hindsight, what valuable life lessons did you learn through that experience?

_____

_____

_____

_____

2. Share a time when failure built the strength of character and resilience in your life.

_____

_____

_____

Proverbs 24:16 GNT:
*"No matter how often honest people fall, they always get up again; but disaster destroys the wicked."*

## **Reflection Questions:**

1. How have you handled failure in your life?

_____
_____
_____
_____

2. In what ways have you been able to overcome failure and learn from your experiences?

_____
_____
_____
_____

## **Action Step:**

1. Reflect on some failures you have experienced in life. What lessons did you learn as a result? Is there a lesson you can share with others?

_____
_____
_____
_____

*Prayer:*
*Lord, thank You for teaching me to see the good that can come out of failure. Thank You for the growth I can see in my life as a result of both my failures and successes. Amen.*

TWENTY-ONE

# Compromise

Proverbs 25:26 TLB:
*"If a godly man compromises with the wicked, it is like polluting a fountain or muddying a spring."*

Compromise can be a weakening or a giving up of our principles or ideals for reasons of expediency. Expediency is doing or considering what is selfish rather than what is right or just. Compromise is a slow process. Compromise is a thousand small concessions in the heart and mind that eventually wear away the truth.

## Discussion Questions:

1. Have you developed a core set of beliefs and values? Why or why not?

_____

_____

_____

_____

2. When faced with the pressure to compromise, how have you been able to stand for what you believe in?

_____

_____

_____

_____

## Psalm 119:3 NLT:
*"They do not compromise with evil, and they walk only in his paths."*

### Reflection Questions:

1. Have you allowed spiritual compromise to creep into your life in some way?

_____

_____

_____

_____

2. Think about how you can stop compromising spiritually in your life.

_____

_____

_____

_____

### Action Step:

1. If you haven't already done so, take time to reflect and meditate on what values and core beliefs you hold dear to your heart. Write down those values and beliefs and make a decision to live by them.

_____

_____

_____

_____

Notes From My Father:

*Prayer:*
*Jesus, help me stand firm in what I believe in. I do not want to compromise my beliefs or core values to please others. Give me the strength and fortitude to live out those beliefs daily. Amen.*

TWENTY-TWO

# Excellence

Daniel 6:3 ESV:
*"Then this Daniel became distinguished above all the other high officials and satraps, because an excellent spirit was in him."*

Excellence can be defined as the quality of being outstanding or extremely good. Biblically speaking, excellence refers to pursuing and doing the best we can with the gifts and abilities God gives us. The spirit of excellence doesn't mean being perfect, but simply giving your best effort.

## Discussion Questions:

1. When you hear the term "spirit of excellence," how do you define it?

_____

_____

_____

_____

2. Are there areas in your life where you display a spirit of excellence? Discuss some of those areas.

_____

_____

_____

_____

Colossians 3:23 GNT:

*"Whatever you do, work at it with all your heart, as though you were working for the Lord and not for people."*

## Reflection Questions:

1. Of the qualities of spiritual excellence mentioned, which ones do you excel in?

_____

_____

_____

_____

2. Which ones do you need to work on?

_____

_____

_____

_____

## Action Step:

1. Pray and ask the Lord what areas you need to improve and decide to start walking in excellence.

_____

_____

_____

_____

Notes From My Father:

*Prayer:*
*Lord, I desire to walk in excellence. Help me do my best in every situation I face. Help me have excellence in every area of my life and help me steward the gifts and abilities You have given me with excellence. Amen.*

# Part V

---

## THE MIND, HEART, AND MOUTH

# The Mind

TWENTY-THREE

# The Mind

Proverbs 23:7 NKJV:
*"For as he thinks in his heart, so is he…"*

According to Scripture, the mind is more than just your thoughts. It is "a way of thinking," a mind attitude, the sum total of the whole mental and moral state of being. Our minds and thinking patterns are shaped by our circumstances, our life experiences, and what was passed down to us by our parents.

## Discussion Questions:

1. Do you agree with the statement the author makes that the way we see and talk to ourselves determines our reality? Why or why not?

_____

_____

_____

_____

2. What strongholds were formed in your childhood? What patterns of thought did you grow up with?

_____
_____
_____
_____

Matthew 15:11 TLB:
*"You aren't made unholy by eating nonkosher food!* **It is what you say and think** *that makes you unclean."*

Matthew 15:18 ERV:
*"But the bad things people say with their mouth come from the way they think. And that's what can make people wrong."*

**Reflection Questions:**

1. How do you talk to and about yourself?

_____
_____
_____
_____

2. How do you think the way you talk to yourself has affected your life?

_____
_____
_____
_____

**Action Step:**

1. Pray and ask the Holy Spirit to identify any negative thought patterns you may have and ask Him to help you renew your mind in those areas.

_____
_____
_____
_____

*Prayer:*

*Father, I come to You in Jesus' name, and I thank You for bringing me into a right relationship with You. As Your child, I ask You to reveal to me any thought patterns holding me back. Thank You for the power of the Holy Spirit to enable me to break those negative thought patterns. I choose to renew my mind with Your Word. In Jesus' name, I pray. Amen.*

TWENTY-FOUR

# Renewing Your Mind

Romans 12:2 NLT:

*"Don't copy the behavior and customs of this world, but let God transform you into a new person by changing the way you think. Then you will learn to know God's will for you, which is good and pleasing and perfect."*

According to Romans 12:2, renewing your mind simply means we interpret life through the lens of God's Word and the inspiration of the Holy Spirit rather than through the lens of our experience, wounds, trauma, or the opinions of others. We must renew our minds with the Word of God and replace the wrong thought patterns we developed. Renewing our minds is a shift toward seeing the world, yourself, and others from a kingdom perspective.

## Discussion Questions:

1. Discuss the meaning of what the author wrote about renewing your mind. Do you see life through the lens of God's Word in every circumstance you face?

_____

_____

_____

_____

2. Discuss what taking a thought captive means. Do your thoughts agree with what God says about you in His Word?

_____

_____

_____

_____

Philippians 4:8 ERV:

*"Brothers and sisters, continue to think about what is good and worthy of praise. Think about what is true and honorable and right and pure and beautiful and respected."*

### Reflection Questions:

1. Have you renewed your mind to such a state that you can easily detect a lie from the enemy and replace it with the truth found in God's Word? What do you need to do moving forward?

_____

_____

_____

_____

2. How well do you do in taking a thought captive?

_____

_____

_____

_____

### Action Step:

1. When a lie from the enemy comes to your mind, speak out loud the Scriptures and reinforce the truth of God's Word over your mind.

_____

_____

_____

_____

Notes From My Father:

*Prayer:*
*Lord, I choose this day to spend time in Your Word and hide the Word in my heart. I choose this day to renew my mind and change my thought patterns. Show me the negative thinking patterns I have developed and help me break the power of those thoughts that have held me back from living the life You desire me to live. Amen.*

TWENTY-FIVE

# Strongholds and Vain Imaginations

2 Corinthians 10:4−5 Voice:

*"The weapons of the war we're fighting are not of the world but are powered by God and effective at tearing down the strongholds erected against His truth. We are demolishing arguments and ideas, every high-and-mighty philosophy that pits itself against the knowledge of the one true God. We are taking prisoners of every thought, every emotion, and subduing them into obedience to the Anointed One."*

Strongholds. Strongholds come from our thoughts. They can develop from our patterns of thinking, our imaginations, or anything that has entered our minds and has been pondered and thought about. A stronghold is a way of thinking and feeling that has developed over time in a person's life.

A stronghold can start from any way thoughts pass through our minds. Strongholds are targeted at our minds. Our real problems are not the trials and problems we go through, but rather what we believe and where we put our faith and trust during problems.

## Discussion Questions:

1. Discuss how we can tear down strongholds in our thinking.

_____

_____

_____

_____

2. What is a vain imagination?

_____

_____

_____

_____

Philippians 4:8 ERV:

_"Brothers and sisters, continue to think about what is good and worthy of praise. Think about what is true and honorable and right and pure and beautiful and respected."_

## Reflection Questions:

1. What you think about matters. Do you find your thoughts are mostly negative or positive?

_____

_____

_____

_____

2. Do you ever think about what you are thinking about?

_____

_____

_____

_____

3. What strongholds in your thinking need to be torn down and replaced with the Word of God?

_____

_____

_____

## **Action Step:**

1. Ask the Holy Spirit to reveal to you any strongholds you have in your thinking and ask Him to help you tear down those strongholds.

_____

_____

_____

_____

———

*Prayer:*

*Jesus, reveal to me areas in my thinking that have become strongholds. Holy Spirit, help me tear down those strongholds. I want to be free from the strongholds that have built up in my mind. Amen.*

# The Heart

TWENTY-SIX

# Guard Your Heart

Proverbs 4:23 NLT:
*"Guard your heart above all else, for it determines the course of your life."*

Merriam-Webster Dictionary describes the heart as one's innermost character, feelings, or inclinations. The heart is your authentic self - the core of your being. The heart is where all our dreams, desires, and passions live. It is the part of you that connects with God and other people.

The Bible tells us to guard and protect our hearts, because from the heart flows the issues of life. We are instructed to keep our heart, meaning we are to watch over it, cultivate it, and protect it.

## Discussion Questions:

1. Discuss what guarding your heart means to you.

_____

_____

_____

_____

2. Has there been a time when you did not guard your heart? What was the result?

_____

_____

_____

_____

Philippians 4:7 NIV:

*"And the peace of God, which transcends all understanding, will guard your hearts and your minds in Christ Jesus."*

## Reflection Question:

1. How well do you think you guard your heart?

_____

_____

_____

_____

## Action Step:

1. Ask the Holy Spirit to shine His light on any area of your heart that needs to be guarded and protected.

_____

_____

_____

_____

*Prayer:*

*Holy Spirit, thank You for showing me where I need to guard and protect my heart. Thank You for helping me to be all You have planned for me to be. Amen.*

# TWENTY-SEVEN

# Bitterness, Rage, and Anger

Ephesians 4:31 Voice:
*"Banish bitterness, rage and anger, shouting and slander, and any and all malicious thoughts-these are poison."*

Bitterness is defined as anger and disappointment at being treated unfairly. It is synonymous with resentment and envy. We all must deal with unforgiveness and bitterness at times in our lives.

**Discussion Questions:**

1. According to what Dr. Steve wrote, where does bitterness take root?

_____

_____

_____

_____

2. Discuss a time when you have been treated unjustly. Were you able to forgive?

_____

_____

_____

_____

Hebrews 12:15 Voice:

*"Watch carefully that no one falls short of God's favor, that no well of bitterness springs up to trouble you and throw many others off the path."*

## Reflection Questions:

1. Are there hurts in your life that you have not dealt with properly?

_____

_____

_____

_____

2. If there are, how can you deal with them now and get free from bitterness?

_____

_____

_____

_____

## Action Step:

1. Write down those who have hurt you. Pray for them, forgive them, and release any hurt and bitterness toward them.

_____

_____

_____

_____

*Prayer:*
*Jesus, I repent for holding bitterness and unforgiveness in my heart toward*
_____ . *By faith, I choose to forgive them. Forgive me for holding onto bitterness and unforgiveness in my heart and release me from the pain and hurt I have carried. Help me be quick to forgive. In Your name, I pray. Amen.*

TWENTY-EIGHT

# Physical Dangers of Bitterness

Proverbs 14:20 AMPC:
*"A calm and undisturbed mind and heart are the life and health of the body, but envy, jealousy, and wrath are like rottenness to the bones."*

Resentment and bitterness are powerful emotions that can consume us from the inside out. We don't often think about the physical dangers of holding onto resentment and bitterness and how it affects our bodies. Resentment and bitterness can increase stress levels and release stress hormones like cortisol and adrenaline. When you harbor these emotions, they can lead to high blood pressure, an increased heart rate, and a weakened immune system.

## Discussion Questions:

1. In what ways do you struggle with bitterness?

_____

_____

_____

_____

2. How has your health been affected by resentment and bitterness?

_____

_____

_____

_____

Ephesians 4:31–32 Philips:
*"Let there be no more resentment, no more anger or temper, no more violent self-assertiveness, no more slander and no more malicious remarks, Be kind to each other, be understanding. Be as ready to forgive others as God for Christ's sake has forgiven you."*

## Reflection Questions:

1. Take some time to reflect and ask yourself if resentment and bitterness have affected your health.

_____

_____

_____

_____

2. Is there someone you hold in bitterness and resentment? If so, release and forgive them and ask the Lord to bless them.

_____

_____

_____

_____

## Action Step:

1. Ask the Holy Spirit to search your heart and reveal to you any areas where you hold on to resentment and bitterness. Then pray and ask Him to release those emotions and receive forgiveness.

_____

_____

_____

_____

Notes From My Father:

*Prayer:*
*Lord, I forgive and release those who have hurt me and caused me harm. I let go of resentment and bitterness that resides in my heart. I thank You that I am free from offense and my health is restored. Amen.*

# TWENTY-NINE

# Unforgiveness

1 John 2:9 GNT:

*"If we say that we are in the light, yet hate others, we are in the darkness to this very hour."*

Unforgiveness is another poison that will infect our lives. Anger, resentment, and bitterness are all fruits of unforgiveness. Unforgiveness is not having the compassion to forgive someone who has offended us, and we *choose* not to be willing to forgive them.

### Discussion Questions:

1. What doors to the devil do you think have been opened in your life because of unforgiveness?

_____

_____

_____

_____

2. Do you have any unresolved issues with others that have caused you to become bitter?

_____

_____

_____

_____

### Mark 11:25 Easy:

*"But when you stand up to pray, first you must forgive other people. If anyone has done something bad against you, forgive that person. If you do forgive them, your Father in heaven will forgive you. God will forgive you for the bad things that you have done."*

## Reflection Questions:

1. Take some time to examine your heart. Are there any offenses you refuse to let go of?

_____

_____

_____

_____

2. Are there people you have *chosen* not to forgive? What does God's Word say about that?

_____

_____

_____

_____

## Action Step:

1. Write down those who you have not forgiven, then pray and, by faith, forgive them.

_____

_____

_____

_____

Notes From My Father:

*Prayer:*

*Father, I come to You in Jesus' name. I want to be free from the bondage that unforgiveness has kept me in. By faith, I now choose to forgive_____. I release them and choose to bless them today. Father, I ask that You break the power the enemy has held in my life because of unforgiveness. Thank You, Jesus, for setting me free today. I choose to walk in forgiveness from this day forward. I pray in Jesus' name. Amen.*

THIRTY

# Forgiving Others

Ephesians 4:32 Voice:

*"Instead, be kind and compassionate. Graciously forgive one another just as God has forgiven you through the Anointed, our Liberating King."*

When we talk about guarding our hearts, we must speak about forgiveness. Both giving forgiveness and receiving forgiveness as well. Sometimes, forgiveness can feel like a unilateral contract. We are doing all the work while the other person gets off free. Refusing to forgive flows from a desire to right a wrong, to make sure we are exonerated, and the other person pays.

**Discussion Questions:**

1. Do you find it easy to be quick to forgive? Why or why not?

_____

_____

_____

_____

2. Are you a person who holds a grudge against someone for something they did long ago?

_____

_____

_____

_____

Colossians 3:13–14 MSG:

*"So, chosen by God for this new life of love, dress in the wardrobe God picked out for you: compassion, kindness, humility, quiet strength, discipline. Be even-tempered, content with second place, quick to forgive an offense. Forgive as quickly and completely as the Master forgave you. And regardless of what else you put on, wear love. It's your basic, all-purpose garment. Never be without it."*

**Reflection Question:**

1. Take some time to reflect on your life and relationships. Are there hurts you are holding on to because you feel you have the right to?

_____

_____

_____

_____

**Action Step:**

1. Ask the Holy Spirit what He wants you to do in this moment, and then obey what He says to do.

_____

_____

_____

_____

*Prayer:*
*Father, I want to be a person who is quick to forgive. I need Your help today to forgive others. Thank You, Jesus, for hearing and answering my prayer. Amen.*

THIRTY-ONE

# Receiving Forgiveness

1 John 1:9 Voice:

*"But if we own up to our sins, God shows that He is faithful and just by forgiving us our sins and purifying us from the pollution of all the bad things we have done."*

To be forgiven by God means our sins have been removed and restoration has taken place. The Lord is faithful, dependable, and trustworthy, and He is always willing and able to forgive us for our sins when we go to Him and confess them and ask for forgiveness.

**Discussion Questions:**

1. Discuss what it means to receive forgiveness by faith. What does that mean to you?

_____

_____

_____

_____

2. Is receiving forgiveness based on feeling? Why or why not?

_____

_____

_____

3. In what ways do you sometimes feel you have to earn God's forgiveness?

_____

_____

_____

_____

### Psalm 32:1−2 TLB:

*"What happiness for those whose guilt has been forgiven! What joys when sins are covered over! What relief for those who have confessed their sins and God has cleared their record."*

## Reflection Question:

1. Has there been a time when you ran from God because of sin rather than turning to Him and receiving forgiveness? Describe what happened.

_____

_____

_____

_____

## Action Step:

1. Receive God's forgiveness by faith today and allow the Word of God to permeate your spirit, soul, and body. Receive peace today.

_____

_____

_____

_____

*Prayer:*
*Help me, Lord, to keep my eyes on You. I thank You that no matter what situation I may face, I can always come to the throne of grace and receive forgiveness and cleansing. Thank You, Jesus. Amen.*

## THIRTY-TWO

# Forgiving Ourselves

Romans 8:1 God's Word:
*"So those who are believers in Christ Jesus can no longer be condemned."*

With forgiveness, the most difficult aspect is forgiving ourselves. While it is the most difficult, it is also the most important. If we cannot forgive ourselves, we will continue to live a life full of condemnation, shame, and guilt.

Forgiving yourself allows you to release the feelings of guilt, shame, and self-blame. It frees you from the negative emotions that can keep you stuck in the past, enabling you to heal and move forward. When we forgive ourselves, we are giving ourselves the gift of freedom.

### Discussion Questions:

1. Do you find it hard to forgive yourself?

_____

_____

_____

_____

2. Discuss what the author writes about an area that has been healed and an area that has not been healed. Have you experienced what the author wrote about in your personal life?

_____

_____

_____

_____

Philippians 3:13–14 Philips:

_"Yet, my brothers, I do not consider myself to have "arrived" spiritually, nor do I consider myself already perfect. But I keep going on, grasping ever more firmly that purpose for which Christ grasped me. My brothers, I do not consider myself to have fully grasped it even now. But I do concentrate on this: **I leave the past behind** and with hands outstretched to whatever lies ahead I go straight for the goal—my reward the honour of being called by God in Christ."_

**Reflection Questions:**

1. Think about an area of your heart that has been healed. Has the sting of that been removed?

_____

_____

_____

_____

2. Think about an area of your heart that hasn't been healed. Do you carry the guilt and shame associated with that?

_____

_____

_____

_____

## **Action Step:**

1. Bring those unhealed areas of your heart to the Lord and ask Him to forgive you and release you from the guilt, condemnation, and shame.

_____

_____

_____

_____

*Prayer:*

*Lord, I thank You for what You have done in my life. Thank You for the areas of my heart You have healed and made whole. There are other areas of my heart that I haven't brought to You. I bring them to you now, and I ask that You forgive me for_____ and release me from the guilt, condemnation, and shame that I have carried. Thank You, Jesus. Amen.*

## THIRTY-THREE

# Humility
_____

Proverbs 22:4 TLB:
*"True humility and respect for the Lord lead a man to riches, honor, and long life."*

Humility is freedom from pride or arrogance; the quality of being humble. Humility is an important characteristic to develop. Being humble means we acknowledge we are completely dependent on God. True humility means we are not scrambling for power, prestige, and position.

The author shares what a dearly beloved pastor once said, "God resists the proud. When I wake up in the morning, if I do not acknowledge God and humble myself before Him, He resists me. But if I humble myself before Him, He can shower me with His grace throughout my day."

## **Discussion Questions:**

1. Discuss what the author means about humility and submission going hand in hand. What does that mean to you?

_____

_____

_____

_____

2. Do you have an area in your life where you are prideful? Do you think God is resisting you?

_____

_____

_____

_____

Colossians 3:12–14 MSG:

*"So, chosen by God for this new life of love, dress in the wardrobe God picked out for you: compassion, kindness, humility, quiet strength, discipline. Be even-tempered, content with second place, quick to forgive an offense. Forgive as quickly and completely as the Master forgave you. And regardless of what else you put on, wear love. It's your basic, all-purpose garment. Never be without it."*

## Reflection Question:

1. Think and reflect on where you are in your life in the area of humility. Is there an area in your heart that you need to submit to God?

_____

_____

_____

_____

## Action Step:

1. Write down what the Holy Spirit reveals to you about pride and pray over those areas.

_____

_____

_____

_____

*Prayer:*

*Father, I confess that I have not walked in humility. I confess I have walked in pride and ask You now to forgive me. I thank You that my sins are forgiven in Jesus' name. Amen.*

# THIRTY-FOUR

## Purity

Matthew 5:8 TLB:
*"Happy are those whose hearts are pure, for they shall see God."*

How can you define purity? Purity can mean to be without malice, evil intent, and sincerity. Being pure in heart involves having a singleness of heart toward God. A pure heart has no hypocrisy, no guile, no hidden motives. The pure heart is marked by transparency and an uncompromising desire to please God in all things.

### Discussion Questions:

1. What is the best way to develop a pure heart?

_____

_____

_____

_____

2. How does watching our words help us develop a pure heart?

_____

_____

_____

_____

Psalm 51:10 GNT:
*"Create a pure heart in me, O God, and put a new and loyal spirit in me."*

## Reflection Questions:

1. As you reflect on your walk with the Lord, would you say you have a pure heart?

_____

_____

_____

_____

2. Where do you need to improve?

_____

_____

_____

_____

## Action Step:

1. Ask the Holy Spirit to develop a pure heart that is clean, blameless, and without guilt.

_____

_____

_____

_____

*Prayer:*
*Father, I thank You for giving me the desire to walk in purity. Do a deep work in my heart, Lord, and change me; in Jesus' name, I pray. Amen.*

THIRTY-FIVE

# Having a Teachable Spirit

Psalm 119:34 AMP:
*"Give me understanding (a teachable heart and the ability to learn), that I may keep Your law; And observe it with all my heart."*

One of our hearts' most critical issues is having a teachable spirit. A person with a teachable spirit is humble, knowing they do not know everything, and has a passion for learning.

It is important for our growth as Christians to cultivate a teachable spirit. We cultivate a teachable spirit by consecrating our lives to the Lord daily and having an ongoing intimate relationship with Him. Being teachable is the key to becoming a great man or woman of God and fulfilling God's destiny for you.

**Discussion Questions:**

1. What do you think the connection is between humility and having a teachable spirit?

_____

_____

_____

_____

2. Discuss how we can cultivate a teachable spirit in our lives.

_____

_____

_____

_____


### Mark 4:25 AMP:

*"For whoever has [a teachable heart], to him more [understanding] will be given; and whoever does not have [a yearning for truth], even what he has will be taken away from him."*

## Reflection Question:

1. Is there an area of pride in your heart that keeps you from being teachable? If so, write them down and bring them before the Lord.

_____

_____

_____

_____


## Action Step:

1. Ask the Holy Spirit what He would have you do in this area of having a teachable spirit.

_____

_____

_____

_____


*Prayer:*
*Father, I humble myself before You, and I ask and desire that You give me a teachable spirit. Teach me Your ways, Lord, and help me understand Your Word. Amen.*

# THIRTY-SIX

## Love
___

1 Corinthians 13:8 Phillips:
*"Love knows no limit to its endurance, no end to its trust, no fading of its hope; it can outlast anything."*

L ove. People. Love people unconditionally. This is a difficult subject to write about and can be one of the most difficult things to cultivate in our hearts.

### **Discussion Questions:**

1. The author talks about biblical love not being an emotion but a decision. What does this mean to you?

_____

_____

_____

_____

2. What are some ways you can show love to people?

_____

_____

_____

_____

3. Do you find it difficult to love people who have hurt you? Why or why not?

_____

_____

_____

_____

### Ephesians 5:1–2 AMP:

*"Therefore become imitators of God [copy Him and follow His example], as well-beloved children [imitate their father]; and walk continually in love [that is, value one another— practice empathy and compassion, unselfishly seeking the best for others], just as Christ also loved you and gave Himself up for us, an offering and sacrifice to God [slain for you, so that it became] a sweet fragrance."*

## Reflection Question:

1. What are some ways you can begin to change and walk in love toward others?

_____

_____

_____

_____

## Action Step:

1. Think of someone who has hurt you. Ask God to show you how you can show love to them.

_____

_____

_____

_____

*Prayer:*

*Jesus, I want to love like You love. Give me Your heart for people. Let me see people through Your eyes. Help me, Holy Spirit, to develop the fruit of love in my life. Thank You, Jesus. Amen.*

THIRTY-SEVEN

# Guarding Your Heart

Proverbs 4:23 NOG:
*"Guard your heart more than anything else, because the source of your life flows from it."*

The Bible tells us to guard our hearts because not doing so can cause great difficulties for us. We must do something if we are going to control and protect our hearts. The things in our hearts will drive our actions. What we store in our hearts will come out of our mouths.

**Discussion Questions:**

1. How do you think meditating on the Word of God daily will protect your heart?

_____

_____

_____

_____

2. Discuss how you can guard your heart by controlling your tongue. What does that mean to you?

_____

_____

_____

_____

### 1 Peter 3:10 GW:

*"People who want to live a full life and enjoy good days must keep their tongues from saying evil things, and their lips from speaking deceitful things."*

## Reflection Question:

1. The author talks about controlling your tongue. Are you careful about the words that come out of your mouth?

_____

_____

_____

_____

## Action Step:

1. After reflecting on your words, make a plan to be more conscious of what you are saying.

_____

_____

_____

_____

*Prayer:*
*Thank You for helping me keep watch over my heart to guard and protect it. Thank You for helping me control my tongue and choose the words I say carefully. Amen.*

# The Mouth

THIRTY-EIGHT

# The Mouth

Matthew 12:34b TLB:
*"…For a man's heart determines his speech."*

What is in your heart will come out of your mouth. In the Bible, the mouth symbolizes speech, communication, and power. It is often associated with blessing and cursing and emphasizes the power of our words to bring life or destruction.

Like it or not, there is a connection between what is in our hearts and what comes from our mouths. If you want to know what is in your heart, watch what comes out of your mouth. What I believe is a product of what I think and believe in my heart. What I believe is revealed by my mouth.

## Discussion Questions:

1. The author writes that what we say is important and will set the course for our life. Do you agree with this? Why or why not?

_____

_____

_____

_____

2. What do you think is the connection between your heart and your mouth?

_____

_____

_____

_____

Ephesians 4:29 GW:

*"Don't say anything that would hurt another person. Instead, speak only what is good so that you can give help wherever it is needed. That way, what you say will help those who hear you."*

### Reflection Questions:

1. Are the words that come out of your mouth faith-filled or negative?

_____

_____

_____

_____

2. What can you do today to change the words you say?

_____

_____

_____

_____

### Action Step:

1. Ask the Holy Spirit to help you be attentive to what comes out of your mouth.

_____

_____

_____

_____

Notes From My Father:

*Prayer:*
*Help me set a guard over my mouth, Lord. Help me change what comes out of my mouth.*
*May I use my mouth to bless and not curse others. Amen.*

THIRTY-NINE

# Words and Their Power

Proverbs 18:21 CEV:
*"Words can bring life or death! Talk too much, and you will eat everything you say."*

Words are powerful. As the Scriptures say, they can bring either life or death. The author writes that the Holy Spirit constantly speaks to him about the words that come out of his mouth. The truth is our words have an impact.

Words not only impact us and how we see ourselves, but they impact others as well. Scientific studies have shown that positive and negative words not only affect us on a deep psychological level, but they significantly impact the outcome of our lives.

## Discussion Questions:

1. Describe what affect words have had on your life.

_____

_____

_____

_____

2. Do you speak positive words to and over yourself?

_____

_____

_____

_____

Proverbs 13:3 NET:

*"The one who guards his words guards his life; whoever is talkative will come to ruin."*

## Reflection Questions:

1. Are the words you speak more positive or negative?

_____

_____

_____

_____

2. What impact do you think your words have over your children?

_____

_____

_____

_____

## Action Step:

1. Be conscious of the words that come out of your mouth. If you tend to be negative, make a commitment to say positive words each day. Look at things in a positive light.

_____

_____

_____

Notes From My Father:

*Prayer:*

*Lord, help me keep watch over my tongue. Remind me to only speak positive words over myself and my children. Reveal to me by Your Spirit, the impact the words I speak have on my family and children. Amen.*

FORTY

# Talking to Yourself

Ephesians 4:29 MSG:
*"Watch the way you talk. Let nothing foul or dirty come out of your mouth. Say only what helps, each word a gift."*

The words we say to ourselves are important and will shape our lives and destinies. The words we say to ourselves are mostly shaped by our experiences, as well as what others have said to or about us. Comments said to us as children can stick with us long enough that they become ingrained in our mindsets as adults. What we hear will have the greatest impact on our lives.

**Discussion Questions:**

1. Have the words that have been spoken over your life brought life or death?

_____

_____

_____

_____

2. Do you agree with the author that you have the power to change your words?

_____

_____

_____

_____

Proverbs 18:21 ERV:
*"The tongue can speak words that bring life or death. Those who love to talk must be ready to accept what it brings."*

## Reflection Questions:

1. What impact have the words that have been spoken to you and over you had?

_____

_____

_____

_____

2. Have you renewed your mind with the Word of God in those areas?

_____

_____

_____

_____

## Action Step:

1. Ask the Holy Spirit to help you identify the negative impact that words others have spoken to you that have become ingrained in your thinking. By the power of the Holy Spirit, break those strongholds in your thinking and replace those words with the Word of God.

_____

_____

_____

_____

Notes From My Father:

*Prayer:*

*Thank You, Lord, for helping me to identify the negative thought patterns that have affected my life. I declare that those negative thought patterns are torn down now in Jesus' Name, and the power of those patterns has been destroyed. I choose to renew my mind with the Word of God and speak the Word out of my mouth. Amen.*

FORTY-ONE

# Talking to Others

Ephesians 4:29 NIV:
*"Do not let any unwholesome talk come out of your mouths, but only what is helpful for building others up according to their needs, that it may benefit those who listen."*

W hat do we say about others? Are we constantly running others down with our words? Have you ever known someone who constantly says negative things about someone else? What do you say about others? Do we backbite and gossip about others?

**Discussion Questions:**

1. How do you talk to and about others? Do you backbite and gossip, or do you bless others with your words?

_____

_____

_____

_____

2. Discuss the impact of your words as it relates to your circle of influence. Do you have a positive impact on others with your words?

_____

_____

_____

_____

## Proverbs 16:24 EHV:

_"Pleasant speech is honey from a honeycomb, sweet to the spirit and healing for the bones."_

### Reflection Question:

1. How can you use your tongue to bless and speak well of others?

_____

_____

_____

_____

### Action Step:

1. Make it a priority to be an encouragement to others with the words you speak. Find something positive to say to each person you come across each day.

_____

_____

_____

_____

_Prayer:_
_Father, I want to use my tongue for good. I want to be an encouragement to someone today._
_Help me find something positive to say to every person who comes across my path today._
_Amen._

# About the Author

Dr. Steve has been a Christ-follower since 1987, when he was miraculously delivered from drug addiction. He has served as a missionary with Go To Nations since 1995.

He has been a full-time missionary, itinerant Bible school teacher, and minister and has traveled all over the world, training emerging leaders.

He lived in Asia for ten years, traveling and teaching in Bible schools in Thailand, Vietnam, India, the Philippines, Malaysia, and Cambodia.

He now lives in Africa with his wife and daughters, ministering in Tanzania and Kenya.

To learn more about Dr. Steve and the ministry he is involved in, please visit these websites:

Go To Nations:
    https://gotonations.org/missionary/wheeler

Dr. Steve's website:
    https://wheelermediagroup.org

Made in the USA
Columbia, SC
01 July 2025

60110148R00098